W9-CJD-145

My First NFL Book

HOUSTON TEXANS

Steven M. Karras

www.av2books.com

Go to **www.av2books.com**, and enter this book's unique code.

BOOK CODE

T776229

AV² **by Weigl** brings you media enhanced books that support active learning.

AV² provides enriched content that supplements and complements this book. Weigl's AV² books strive to create inspired learning and engage young minds in a total learning experience.

Your AV² Media Enhanced books come alive with...

Audio
Listen to sections of the book read aloud.

Video
Watch informative video clips.

Embedded Weblinks
Gain additional information for research.

Try This!
Complete activities and hands-on experiments.

Key Words
Study vocabulary, and complete a matching word activity.

Quizzes
Test your knowledge.

Slide Show
View images and captions, and prepare a presentation.

... and much, much more!

Published by AV² by Weigl
350 5th Avenue, 59th Floor
New York, NY 10118

Website: www.av2books.com

Printed in the United States of America in Brainerd, Minnesota
1 2 3 4 5 6 7 8 9 0 21 20 19 18 17

042017
020317

Editor: Katie Gillespie
Art Director: Terry Paulhus

Weigl acknowledges Getty Images, Alamy, and iStock as the primary image suppliers for this title.

Library of Congress Control Number: 2017930543

ISBN 978-1-4896-5511-0 (hardcover)
ISBN 978-1-4896-5513-4 (multi-user eBook)

Copyright ©2018 AV² by Weigl
All rights reserved. No part of this publication may be reproduced, stored in a retrieval system, or transmitted in any form or by any means, electronic, mechanical, photocopying, recording, or otherwise, without the prior written permission of the publisher.

My First NFL Book

HOUSTON TEXANS

CONTENTS

Team History

The Houston Texans joined the NFL in 2002. They are the newest team in the league. The Texans beat the Dallas Cowboys 19–0 in their first regular season home game. Quarterback David Carr threw the Texans' first touchdown pass to tight end Billy Miller to win that game.

The Texans showed off their team uniforms to 12,000 fans in 2001.

The Stadium

NRG Stadium is the Texans' home field. It is the first stadium of its kind to have a roof that can open and close. Behind one end zone is the Bull Pen. Fans in this area stand for most of the game and cheer loudly.

NRG Stadium is in Houston, Texas. It is also home to the Houston Livestock Show and Rodeo.

Team Spirit

The Texans' mascot is a bull named Toro. *Toro* means "bull" in Spanish. His favorite songs are "Wooly Bully" and "Deep in the Heart of Texas." Toro sometimes slides down a rope from the top of NRG Stadium down to the stands.

Toro likes to eat chips with salsa.

The Jerseys

The Texans' team colors are called Deep Steel Blue, Battle Red, and Liberty White. The players wear blue jerseys for home games and white jerseys for away games. There is one Battle Red Day each year when the players wear red jerseys.

The Helmet

The Texans' helmets are dark blue with the Texans' logo on each side. The logo is in the shape of a bull's head. It is red, white, and blue with a white star. The star is called the Lone Star. This is a symbol of the state of Texas.

Plastic helmets with padding inside replaced leather helmets in the 1950s.

The Coach

Bill O'Brien became the Texans' head coach in 2014. O'Brien played college football. He also coached college football and worked for the New England Patriots. O'Brien had the most wins of any Texans coach in their first two seasons.

Player Positions

A cornerback is part of the defense. This player's job is to stop the other team's offense from catching passes. Cornerbacks have to be fast. They also have to be able to tackle other players.

The Texans' first cornerback was signed to the team on December 29, 2001.

J.J. Watt plays defensive end for the Texans. He was drafted to the team in 2011. Watt led the NFL in sacks in both 2012 and 2015. A sack is when a defensive player tackles the other team's quarterback. Watt has been named the NFL Defensive Player of the Year three times.

Andre Johnson was a wide receiver. He had 10 or more catches and ran 100 or more receiving yards in 20 different games. This is an NFL record. Johnson was named the team's Most Valuable Player four times. He had 1,012 catches, 13,597 yards, and 64 touchdowns. This makes him the Texans' all-time leading receiver.

Team Records

The Texans set a team record for most points scored in a game when they beat the Tennessee Titans 45–21 in 2014. Arian Foster holds the team record for most rushing yards. He had 1,454. Matt Schaub made a team record of 1,951 passes in his career.

45 Points Scored in One Game

Arian Foster

1,454 Rushing Yards

Matt Schaub

1,951 Passes

21

By the Numbers

The Texans are the **32ⁿᵈ** team to join the NFL.

Lineman Chester Pitts started in **114** straight games.

Linebacker Brian Cushing led the team with **133 tackles** in 2009.

The average number of fans at a Texans home game is **71,769**.

NRG Stadium's roof can open in only **7 minutes**.

Kris Brown is the Texans' all-time leading scorer. He made **767 points**.

Quiz

1. Which quarterback threw the Texans' first touchdown pass in their first home game?

2. What does *toro* mean in Spanish?

3. Which Texans player led the NFL in sacks in 2012 and 2015?

4. How many touchdowns did Andre Johnson score in his career?

5. How long does it take for NRG Stadium's roof to open?

ANSWERS 1. David Carr 2. Bull 3. J.J. Watt 4. 64 5. 7 minutes

MEDIA ENHANCED BOOKS
AV2 BY WEIGL™
ADDED VALUE • AUDIO VISUAL

Check out www.av2books.com for activities, videos, audio clips, and more!

The AV² Collection

1 Go to www.av2books.com.

2 Enter book code. T776229

3 Fuel your imagination online!

www.av2books.com